HOW TO GET RICH

Secret to financial stability and easy tips on how to manage your finances

By Rosy Scott

TABLE OF CONTENT

INTRODUCTION

How To Become Rich - It's More Than Millions In The Bank

Learning how to become wealthy might mean being debt free, retiring early, paying off your home, not living paycheck to paycheck, or simply having a positive net worth. What you desire could be radically different from what someone else wants, and that's good.
When I was younger I believed that I wanted a massive home, a pretty nice automobile, and to be able to purchase whatever fashionable things I desired.

To me, it was being affluent.
Now, I know that, to me, being rich means being comfortable - no debt, money in the bank, having a lovely family and spending time doing what I enjoy.

I am lot happy with this life, and I learned that being affluent doesn't imply what I thought it meant.

Whatever your concept of "rich" is, you can transform your life and make your dreams

While many believe finding out how to get wealthy may be difficult, I'm here to tell you that you may attain your ambitions. Trust me, when I began my blog, I had no notion that blogs could produce money. I didn't know what I was doing and learned along the way.

If you want to attain financial success (whatever that may mean to you) one day, then you'll have to start by adopting solid financial habits today. You will have to work hard, be better than average, and be ready to work outside of the norm.
Learning how to become wealthy won't be simple (particularly if you want to learn how

to get rich overnight) – but what good things come easily anyways?

For many individuals, understanding how to get wealthy may seem difficult and entirely unreachable, but that's just not true. Remember, being affluent isn't necessarily about having millions of cash in the bank. Having money or being financially independent may come in various ways. As I stated, you may simply want to aim toward having zero debt.

No matter what your aim is, knowing how to get wealthy is about having the appropriate mentality. Achieving financial success is hard work, but beginning now means you'll be there that much sooner.

If you want to develop your wealth, whatever that may mean to you, then you're going to have to be above average when it comes to your money. That's because the ordinary person struggles with money, and

many are wrecked with worry and misery
owing to their bad financial status.

Here Are Some stunning Money Statistics:

68% of Americans live paycheck to
paycheck.
26% have no emergency savings.
The median amount saved for retirement is
less than $60,000.
The typical family has $7,283 in credit card
debt.
The average student loan debt is $32,264.
To be better than average and to learn how
to become wealthy, you'll have to work hard,
learn how to handle your money better, and
take some risks.

Just remember, being rich doesn't
necessarily mean millions and millions of
money - it's the type of financial satisfaction
and success you need for your life.

Chapter 1

FIRST, DISCOVER HOW TO GET WEALTHY NOW.

I know many individuals who put off preparing for retirement, finding their ideal career, or making adjustments that would bring them financial bliss. I find that most individuals put these tasks off because they assume they have loads of time.

Instead of assuming that you're indestructible and that you have all the time in the world to improve your money, you should stop procrastinating and learn how to alter your financial life immediately.

Many individuals put things off and/or spend their money irresponsibly because they assume they can start tomorrow, start next month, and so on. However, each time you put off fixing your money, you are that much farther away. It becomes harder to work towards your objective when you continually put it off.

Stop wasting time and take charge of your financial condition today.

Reach for your ambitions.
Those who create objectives are considerably more likely to be successful than those who do not. Due to that, if you want to learn how to become wealthy, you'll need to start by creating objectives for yourself.

Setting objectives is vital because without a goal, how do you know where you're heading? Goals may keep you motivated and striving for your best.

When you're establishing plans for a brighter financial future, you should make sure that your aim is SMART.
A SMART goal is:

Specific – What is your goal? Is it specific enough or is it too broad? What needs to be done for you to achieve your goal? Why do you want to reach your goal?
Measurable – How can you measure your progress? How will you know if you're on track?
Attainable – Is this a goal that can be achieved?
Realistic/relevant – Can you achieve your goal? Is the goal worth it?
Time – What's your time frame for reaching your goal?
So, take what being rich means to you and turn it into a goal. But, make sure it meets the standards above.

Even SMART goals can sound huge, so to reach your financial goals and learn how to become rich, you'll want to:

Write down your goals and objectives.
Create a plan to reach your life goals.
Break each goal apart into smaller goals.
Keep track of your goal-setting progress and make changes (if needed).
Find small ways to stick to your goal.
Find ways to motivate yourself when setting goals.
Make reaching your goal a friendly competition.
Manage your money with a budget.

Nearly everyone needs a budget, whether you have a million dollars already in the bank or are working to pay off debt. So, to learn how to become rich, you'll want to create a budget.

Budgets are what help you work towards the financial goals you've just created. And, even when you do reach your goals, a budget will help prevent future financial stress. This is because budgets keep you mindful of your income and expenses. With a budget, you will know exactly how much you can spend in a category each month, how much you have to work with, and what spending areas need to be evaluated, among other things.

However, not many people have a budget. More than 60% of households in the U.S. do not have a budget.

If you are new to budgeting, be sure to include all of your income and expenses when creating your budget.

Here are some expenses you may want to include, but don't forget any expenses you have that aren't listed:

Home – House payment, rent, maintenance, utilities, insurance, property taxes, etc.

Car – Monthly car payment, gas, maintenance, insurance, license plate fees, and so on

Television, cable, Netflix, Hulu, etc.

Cell phone

Internet

Food – Groceries, restaurant spending, snacks, etc.

Clothing

Entertainment – Entertainment can include many things, such as going to the movies, going out for drinks, concert tickets, sports, and so on

Charity – If you regularly donate to charity, then this should be an area you budget for

Savings funds – This can be for your retirement fund, wedding, travel, etc.

Taxes – If you are self-employed, then taxes may consist of a large part of your budget

Health insurance

Miscellaneous – Pet expenses, fees, childcare, school, gifts, etc.

After you know your expenses, balance those with your income – you should be making more than you are spending. A budget can show you how to become rich fast by showing you exactly what needs to be addressed. You may realize there are some things you can cut out, that you can put more in savings than you thought, etc.

Understand that a fun life can be affordable. I do not like the myth that people who save money are boring. That's simply not true at all.

I believe that you can balance living a good life with saving a comfortable amount of money.

There are plenty of ways to live an awesome life while saving money. Yes, you can still see your friends, have fun with your loved ones, go on vacations, and more, all while staying on a realistic budget.

If you want to learn how to become rich, then learning how to be happy with yourself and figuring out affordable ways to enjoy life is key.

Pay off your debt at a high-interest rate. Eliminating your debt will undoubtedly be one of your objectives if you want to discover how to become wealthy. For the normal person, this most likely refers to any debt with a high-interest rate, debt that might be stressing you out, and so forth.

Your stress levels may decrease as a result of paying off your debt, and you'll have more money to spend on other things (such as retirement). Just consider how much more you will need to spend on your objectives if you stop paying excessive interest payments only.

Realizing why you have debt in the first place is the first step in getting rid of it. I think it will be difficult to change for the better if you don't know where your financial problem came from.

Yes, it's fantastic to merely start paying down your debt, but you don't want to keep getting sucked into the vicious loop of incurring debt.

The next stage is to determine how you will get rid of your debt after you have determined why you are in debt (or why you keep getting back into it). There are various strategies to deal with your debt, but I believe the best results come from implementing all of the recommendations below.

You should: get out of debt and discover how to become wealthy.

Stop piling up debt in your life. You might wish to stop using or freeze your credit card(s), think twice before making a purchase, and stay away from places where you could be tempted to overspend, like the mall.

Regarding your income and expenses, be reasonable. If you are in debt, you either have a problem with your income or your expenditure. If you want to figure out how to become wealthy, you might need to start earning more money or cutting back on your spending.

Reduce your expenses and spending. There are a variety of things you could want to give up depending on how soon you want to pay off your debt. You could stop buying Starbucks (I know, I know), spend less at restaurants, work out for less money, trade in your car for something more reasonably priced, cook from scratch, etc.

Earn extra cash. You will have more money to pay off your debt and can typically do so faster if you earn more money.

Don't just pay the minimum. If you have debt, you should always make more than the required minimum payment to reduce your interest costs.

Make small payments on your debt. For instance, you should pay off your debt with an additional $25 you receive (for instance, from selling something). Most likely, you won't even notice missing those meager sums of cash.

Related Article: How to Travel to Hawaii for 10 Days for $22.40, including Flights and Lodging

Get a savings rate that is more than 20 times the average.

Although high-yield savings accounts are a fantastic method to increase your savings, most people keep their money in low-yield accounts. Sadly, that means a lot of you are missing out on some quick money!

If you're like the majority of people, you probably have no idea what interest rate your checking and savings accounts are earning. Because you probably opened the account years ago and forgot what the rate was, that is.

You may begin earning 2.39% with Betterment every day with a balance as low as $0.01.

How does that compare to the national average savings rate? While it's greater than the ones I listed earlier, it's still a very sad 0.09%. That is a HUGE contrast from what Betterment every day is offering. If you are just collecting 0.09%, then you are losing out on easy, passive money.

Savings accounts at brick-and-mortar banks are infamous for having low-interest rates. That's because they have a considerably larger overhead — paying for the facility, paying the tellers, etc. Betterment every day is an online choice, which means they have

cheaper costs than passing the savings on to you.
Over 10 years, that same savings balance with a 2.39% balance would earn you an additional $2,390, whereas a savings account with an interest rate of only 0.09% would earn you a measly $90.

Your money is just as safe in a Betterment Everyday account as it is with a brick-and-mortar bank. You're merely earning extra interest, which is something that everyone seeking to learn how to get rich can take advantage of.

CHAPTER 2

START INVESTING

It may be intimidating, unpleasant, and overwhelming to approach the subject of investing your money. However, you want to invest to:

one day, I will retire.
Prepare for unexpected happenings in the future.
Give your money time to grow.
Learn how to get wealthy.
Starting an investment is often the most difficult aspect. And I fully comprehend that. How do you begin? How much do you put aside? Where do you put the money that you invest?

But the sooner you start investing, the more it becomes second nature and the simpler it is. By investing money today, you will acquire solid investment habits that will assist you long into the future.

Keep in mind that time is on your side and that it can alter your life because of compound interest. This implies that the sooner you invest your money, the more you'll make over time.

Compound interest is defined. When interest is earning interest, you have compound interest. This might make the money you have saved grow into a considerably greater sum in the future.

This is crucial to understand because, if you merely leave $100 sitting in a bank account or beneath a mattress, it won't be worth $100 in the future. However, if you invest, you can increase the value of your $100. Your money is working for you when you invest, potentially generating income for you.

For instance, $1,000 invested in a retirement account with an annual 8% return would be worth $21,724 after 40 years. The same $1,000 would become $301,505 if you invested an additional $1,000 each year for 40 years at an annual return of 8%. If you invested an additional $10,000 for 40 years at an annual return of 8%, the first $10,000 would grow to $3,015,055.

Here are a few simple steps you may follow to begin investing:

Save a portion of your income only for investment. You must start putting aside money particularly for investing before you can begin investing your money. You have complete discretion over how much money you set aside for investments, although in general, the more the better.

Research. It's a good idea to know what you're investing in before you start pouring money into the stock market and other investments. You may get more knowledgeable about your investing choices by reading about different investment-related suggestions and studying each investment, which will then help you make better judgments going forward.

Look for a person or an online brokerage to handle your money. There are primarily two methods for investing money. Either you can manage your investment portfolio via a brokerage firm, or you can find someone to do it for you. To truly begin investing your money, you must engage in one of these activities. I like to do things via Vanguard on my own.

Decide on your investment strategy. You need to choose where you will deposit your assets now that you have a brokerage account. Your choice of investments will rely on your risk tolerance, the length of the

investment horizon (when will you retire?), and other factors. Generally speaking, the longer your period is, the more risk you may be ready to take on, however the sooner you need your money, the less risk you will take on.
Keep an eye on your investment holdings. Tracking your investments regularly is the next stage in learning how to get wealthy via investing. This is crucial since you could ultimately need to alter your investments, add additional funds to them, and so forth. Continue the instructions above over and over again. You should keep doing the aforementioned actions to continue investing for a very long time. It only becomes simpler now that you are aware of the procedures involved in investing your money.

Make additional revenue.
If you want to learn how to become wealthy without having any money, you may need to

come up with techniques to increase your income to become financially independent.

I spend a lot of time on Making Sense of Cents discussing ways to create additional money because I think that doing so may transform your life. You can stop living paycheck to paycheck, you can pay off your debt, and more – all by learning about the many different ways to make money.

Believe me when I say it's crucial to increase your income. I was able to quit my day job to follow my love and travel full-time, pay off $38,000 in school debts in only 7 months, and more!

The beautiful thing about exploring methods to create extra money is that your revenue potential is endless. There is no upper limit to the amount of money you may earn; it all depends on what you choose to accomplish and how much time you are willing to invest in it.

Making more money can change your life in
great ways, such as:

Your debts may be settled.
Save for significant expenditures, such as a
trip.
Stop relying only on your paychecks.
arrive at retirement earlier.
Increase the variety of your income sources.
There are various ways to make additional
money, whether you have one spare hour
per day or are prepared to put in 40 to 50
hours per week in addition to your full-time
employment. Finding methods to create
more money can only benefit you as you
learn how to become affluent.

Some ways to make more money include:

Obtain a part-time position.
You can earn money online by starting a
blog or working as a virtual assistant, for
example.

Maintain and tidy yards. Mowing lawns, eliminating weeds, clearing gutters, raking leaves, and other tasks can all earn you money.

Answer surveys. I suggest American Consumer Opinion, Swagbucks, Survey Junkie, InboxDollars, Pinecone Research, and Opinion Outpost as survey providers. Both joining and using them are free! Survey responses and product testing are both paid for. It's best to sign up for as many as you can as that way you can receive the most surveys and make the most money.

Move furniture and find jobs on Craigslist.

Movers can earn a broad range when it comes to hourly pay, but it's usually somewhere around $50 an hour if you run your own business.

If you like taking care of animals, you may want to consider finding out how to earn additional money by dog walking or pet sitting. With this side business, you may spend a few minutes at your client's

residence each day to check in, you might stay there, or the animals might stay with you. Joining Rover is a great way to start working as a dog walker and pet sitter.
Learn more about this at Rover – A Great Way To Make Money And Play With Animals.
Babysit and/or nanny children.
Sell your stuff.
Rent a spare room in your home to someone else.
As you can see, the list is endless when it comes to making more money. You can learn how to become rich online or offline!

Having multiple sources of income
The wealthy and successful typically have a wide variety of sources of income. According to some reports, the majority of millionaires have seven sources of income.

They may have a day job, a business, rental properties, dividend income, and more. They act in this way because they are aware that one source of income might not be permanent. Additionally, diversifying your sources of income will reduce your financial risks.

If you ever feel too reliant on one source of income, then you know how important this is. You might be worried that your primary source of income will be affected by something or that you will lose your job one day.

If you work to diversify your income and create multiple income streams, you won't be as concerned if something were to happen to one of your income sources.

You will have a backup plan, you may be able to retire more easily, you will learn how to become wealthy, and so on by diversifying your income through multiple income streams.

Finding a side business you can do in addition to your regular job can be a simple way to find a second source of income. Some side hustles are active work, but they can still help you build passive sources of income (like investing) that will help you diversify your income even more.

Note: If you're interested in managing your money better, I suggest you check out Personal Capital, a free service. You can combine your financial accounts with Personal Capital so that you can quickly view your financial situation, cash flow, intricate graphs, and more.

Even the wealthy practice thrift.
One fallacy about affluent individuals is that they all spend loads of money on ridiculous stuff they don't need. That's just not true at all!

Yes, there are tales of wealthy people blowing their money irresponsibly and going bankrupt. Surprisingly, the typical millionaire is thrifty and has good money management skills.

You don't trust me? Examples of millionaires and billionaires who still find ways to save money include the following:

Warren Buffett lives in a home that he acquired in 1958 for roughly $30,000. John Caudwell, who is worth $2.7 billion, commutes 14 miles by bicycle each day to work and even does his hair styling.
The founder's son of Walmart, Jim C. Walton, operates an old truck without air conditioning.
Another intriguing fact is that the typical couponer makes over $100,000 annually. Surprisingly, compared to those with great earnings, individuals who make under $100,000 a year seldom utilize coupons!

Finding strategies to save money can allow you to retain more of your money, discover how to become wealthy, increase your investment returns, and other benefits. You worked hard for your money, so you may as well discover methods to retain more of it!

Don't try to win people over.

If you want to discover how to grow wealthy with no money or education, then you will want to think about your spending selections.

When was the last time you purchased with someone else's approval in mind?

Sadly, the ordinary individual does this rather often.

Stop trying to impress others and start living your own life if you want to start accumulating wealth and learn how to get rich.

Rich people frequently live beyond their means. Yes, many of them continue to live beyond their means, but this isn't the case for all of them. Millionaires often purchase old goods, they drive "average" automobiles like Toyotas, and they don't buy stuff only to impress others.

Those who aren't wealthy find this to be quite different.

Many people try to keep up with others and fall for lifestyle inflation, which can prevent a person from being a good money manager.

When trying to keep up with the Joneses, you might spend money you do not have. You might put expenses on credit cards so that you can (in a pretend world) "afford" things. You might buy things that you do not care about. The issues may never end.

Instead of attempting to seem wealthy, improve your money management skills to become wealthy one day.

It's crucial to understand that you shouldn't constantly try to impress people if you're wondering, "How can I get rich without a job?"

Related: 15 Beginner Financial Book Picks

CHAPTER 3

RECOGNIZE THE WORTH OF YOUR TIME.

I once had a client whose assistant's only responsibility was paying bills when I was still employed as a financial analyst. The assistant simply spent their day keeping track of which bills needed to be paid, like the house's electricity bill.

I initially thought this was absurd. After all, I was struggling to manage my debt and pay my bills, so the idea that someone could afford to hire someone for such a menial task (one that could even be automated) seemed absurd to me.

They probably never received a late payment, though. Additionally, it's possible

that they simply didn't like handling that
aspect of their lives.

Now, I'm not saying you should hire
someone to pay your bills, but you can still
outsource some of your duties so you can
concentrate your time on the things you
value and want to do. By doing this, you can
increase your wealth much more quickly
than someone who rarely or never
outsources.
Some of the work you may wish to outsource
includes:

cleaning your residence.
Mowing your lawn.
Getting your groceries delivered.
Hire an assistant.
Having an expert do your taxes.
And so on.
Before you outsource something, think
about how much it costs you to do that task.
In the time it takes you to do a task, can you
be earning more with your time by doing

something else? Can you hire an expert to save you money or help you make more money on something? Will occasionally outsourcing a task let you spend more time with your family?

This is a rich habit. The wealthy and successful understand the value of their time and use it to their advantage. They don't waste time doing things that they don't see a benefit from.

What is the fastest way to become a millionaire?
The fastest way to learn how to become a millionaire with no money will vary from person to person.

With the tips and advice above, you will be able to see what will work best for you, as well as what you are most interested in. Whether you are looking to learn how to become rich long-term through real estate assets, building a small business and joining the world of entrepreneurs, creating passive income ideas for yourself, having a portfolio of stocks, or something else, there are many ways for you to build wealth.

Yes, this means that there are other ways to become wealthy other than to become a lottery winner or gamble.

If you have any questions, you may benefit from finding a financial adviser who can assist you more with your unique situation, as they can become more acquainted with what is going on in your life, since everyone is different. Your finances and money management may also be improved by working with a financial counselor.

Do you believe that learning how to become wealthy without any money is possible? Do you think of yourself as wealthy? Do you believe it is possible to learn how to become wealthy without having any money?

CHAPTER 4

SIMPLE WAYS TO MANAGE YOUR MONEY BETTER

Making ends meet is just one aspect of excellent money management. It's okay if you're not the best at arithmetic; all you need to know about addition and subtraction are the fundamentals.

When you are financially savvy, life is a lot simpler. Your credit score and the total amount of debt you end up with depending on how you manage your money. Here are some suggestions to help you improve your financial habits if you're suffering from money management challenges like living paycheck to paycheck while earning more than enough money.

Never assume you can afford anything when presented with a financial choice, particularly one involving a large buy. Make sure you can afford it and that you haven't previously used those dollars for another obligation.

This entails determining your ability to finance a purchase using your budget and the balances in your checking and savings accounts. Keep in mind that just because you have the money doesn't imply you can buy what you want. The bills and costs you have to pay before your next paycheck must also be taken into account.

ORGANIZE TO REDUCE YOUR COST OF LIVING

Finances One of the keys to reaching one's financial objectives for many individuals is learning improved money management skills. Don't berate yourself if you haven't managed your money well in the past.

Nobody is born with the ability to handle their money. Just like driving a vehicle or playing an instrument, it's something that has to be learned and perfected through time.

If you want to get your finances under control, it's never too late to start. What follows is a list of fundamental money management skills and some money management strategies you can start adopting into your regular life so you may attain financial independence - whatever that looks like for you.

SET CLEAR FINANCIAL GOALS

Setting up some financial objectives, both large and little, can help you determine whether you're managing your money properly. You will know you are effective at managing your money when you make progress toward these goals, and this knowledge will only inspire you to do even better.

Make critical financial objectives for yourself. Setting specific financial objectives can undoubtedly assist you with your money management, regardless of whether your objective is to open a $500 or $1,000 emergency savings account, settle one credit card, get out of debt, or prepare for a down payment on a house.

Determine the relevance of your objectives once you've written them down, and then estimate how much money you'll need to put aside each month to achieve them in the period you've chosen. Then sit down with your budget and figure out how to set aside the appropriate amount of money each month to achieve each of your objectives.

You may not have the money to work on every objective right now. If a goal is really important to you, you'll eventually find a way to achieve it, even if that means finding a way to increase your income or reduce your expenses. Also keep in mind that achieving one goal, like paying off debt, might free up funds to work toward other objectives.

GET YOUR FINANCES IN ORDER

Organizing your accounts is a crucial, fundamental money management skill that everyone should learn. You're much more likely to miss payment deadlines, hurt your credit, overdraw your bank accounts (because you don't know what your balances are or when all your payments are due), pay steep NSF fees on bounced checks, and spend a lot of time looking for documents if your bills and financial statements aren't organized and readily available.

Even just one location on a desk might be designated in your house for your own money. Purchase the necessary supplies to aid in your organization, such as a file cabinet, boxes, folders, a computer, or whatever works for you. Some individuals even choose to scan crucial papers and save a duplicate of them on their computers as a backup in case the originals are misplaced or destroyed.

You may also make your system simpler if you're having trouble keeping all of your documentation organized by subscribing to online statements. But if you discover that you need to see your invoices to understand when they need to be paid, obtain a different calendar and mark it up with all of your payment dates. Another option is to utilize an online calendar that notifies you through email or text messages.

KNOW HOW TO BUDGET YOUR MONEY

You can create a financial plan to reach your objectives if you have a budget and understand how to manage your money.

Keep track of both the money coming in (such as salary, bonuses, pension, etc.) and the money going out (rent, insurance, living expenses, bill payments).

Look carefully at where your money is going and decide which areas you may cut down on if you find that you are spending more each month than you are earning. The slightest changes—that daily cappuccino, or lunch at a restaurant—can have the largest effects. You may learn how to manage your money by using a budget calculator spreadsheet.

It's a good idea to maintain a spending journal so you can track your spending to make sure your budget is reasonable. For roughly a month, keep a note of everything you spend money on using an expenditure tracker to gain a clear picture of your spending patterns. When you know where your money is going, it will be much easier for you to change your daily spending patterns and stay within your budget.

A budget is necessary for excellent money management since it's critical to just spend the money that is available to you rather than the money that you anticipate earning. Once you've established a budget, you must follow it and use caution while making daily purchases.

Living on a budget essentially means spending less than you make. You won't run the risk of leading an untenable lifestyle and piling up debt if you live within your means.

It won't harm to seek methods to save money as long as you stay within your budget. Use coupons to save money while shopping for groceries and planning your meals around what's on sale at the grocery store. Brew your coffee at home rather than purchasing a latte at the neighboring coffee shop. You may more easily live within your means and within your budget by adopting minor money-saving practices like these. Check out this, this, or this for a ton of fantastic money-saving suggestions.

REDUCE YOUR DEBT

Make a Budget to Better Manage Your Finances

Regardless of whether you choose the avalanche or snowball approach, you must begin paying off your debt. You'll be able to release the financial weight that is keeping you from becoming financially free faster if you pay off your obligations.

If you're having financial trouble, it's normal to feel overwhelmed, and it might be easy to put off reading your bank accounts and responding to collection calls. However, ignoring the issue won't stop the costs from piling up. The greatest thing you can do for yourself and your finances if you're behind on your debt payments or finding it difficult

to make even the minimum payment is to
consult with a certified non-profit credit
counselor. They'll go through your finances
with you, assist you in developing a sensible
budget, and provide you with information
on all of your debt-reduction possibilities.

It took you a while to accumulate debt, and
it will take you just as long to pay it off.
Thus, practice self-compassion. To
permanently eliminate your debt, you must
regularly make your debt payments and
practice responsible credit use.

REGULARLY MAKE SAVINGS

Saving money is probably the last thing on
your mind if you're having trouble paying
off your obligations. You must make plans to
save money for unforeseen expenses right
now. Having emergency funds will stop you
from using credit, which will only cause you
to go further into debt, in the case of an

unforeseen sickness, house repairs, or if you or your spouse loses their job.

You may avoid financial calamity by setting aside some money for savings, and it also helps you achieve your financial objectives. Work with your spending plan to determine whether you have space to make a monthly $20 contribution to an emergency savings account. Your income level, family size, debt load, and financial objectives will all affect how much you should save each month, but it's vital to keep in mind that every little bit counts.

Continue saving until you have enough to cover your costs for three months. If you are unable to save this amount right away, don't worry. Do your best with what you have, but keep it in mind as a goal. Once you begin going, you'll be shocked at how fast your savings may mount up!

Making the most of your current finances is the key to good money management and achieving your long-term financial objectives. You'll be able to pay your living costs, maintain your debts at a reasonable level or pay them off entirely, and save for the luxuries that make life fun if you know how to handle your money.

Make an appointment to chat with one of our qualified, nonprofit credit counselors if money worries are keeping you up at night. They'll be able to assist you in getting your finances under control and moving you closer to developing superior money management skills.